Life Without Furniture

Sharon Fagan McDermott

Cover art: Richard T. Scott
Cover & interior design: Daniel Krawiec

ISBN 978-0-936481-25-8

Library of Congress Control Number: 2018938752

Jacar Press
6617 Deerview Trail
Durham, NC 27712
www.jacarpress.com

Language is the only homeland.

~ Czeslaw Milosz

Now whenever I sit in the bright sunlight, I
contemplate not what passes by
or what comes into view then vanishes,
but the beautiful stillness
and splendor of staying in place;
I think of the many things I never want to have, and then
I stop thinking about them.

~ Jose Padua, "On the Grammar of the Days and
These Evenings of a Million Words"

For my mother— Mary Ellen Fagan—
and my four remarkable sisters— Tricia, Maureen, Kate, and Siobhan—
with deep gratitude for our shared love, inspiration, and support through the years.
You are, each, sanctuary and song in my life.

Acknowledgements

Grateful acknowledgement to the editors of the following journals and anthologies, where poems from this collection first appeared, sometimes in slightly different form.

- *Commonwealth: Poets on Pennsylvania* anthology: "Audubon Nature Preserve, Fox Chapel"
- *Connotations Press*: "Room in Brooklyn, 1932"
- *Eclectica Magazine*: "In the Winter Room;" Summer Prayer, Pennsylvania;" "Prayer to Dylan Thomas;" "Springtime, New Jersey;" "After the Diagnosis;" " Rooms" (as "Short Takes")
- *Eclectica Magazine: Best Poetry, 20 years Online* anthology: "Crows: The Yard"
- *5 AM*: "October"
- *Intimacy*: (anthology, Jacar Press) "Hymn to Constellations"
- *La Fovea*: "Because Desire is Filled with Endless Distances;" "And Sometimes a Bird Wearing Water and Stillness"
- *The Naugatuck River Review*: "Letter to My Father;" "And After We Failed One Another, I Attempt to Define Love Again"
- *Pittsburgh City Paper*: "Aphids, July, Pittsburgh"
- *Pittsburgh Poetry Review*: "Poem in Response to Whitman's "The Million Dead, Too, Summ'd Up"
- *Poem Your Heart Out* anthology: "Hubris"
- *Poet Lore*: "The Body Dreams Itself"
- *Raleigh Review*: "Waiting for Gauguin"
- *The Redheaded Stepchild*: "Longitude"
- *The Seneca Review*: "Crows"
- *Tupelo Quarterly*: "Life Without Furniture"

Additionally, the following poems appeared in earlier chapbooks:

- *Alley Scatting* (Parallel Press, University of Wisconsin-Madison): "Rain, Streetlight;" "No Name Alley."
- *Bitter Acoustic* (Jacar Press, NC): "Against Unraveling;" "Conversation, New Friends, 61-C Café."

With loving thanks to friends and writers who inspired my work along the way: Liz Ahl, Melissa Bender, Ruth Buckley, Toi Derricotte, Barbara Edelman, Lynn Emanuel, Terrance Hayes, Gene Mariani, Kerry Parslow, Nancy Reddy, Ellen McGrath Smith, Margaret Ellen Smith, Judith Sanders, Jean Valentine, Bob Walicki, and Karen Lynn Williams. Deep gratitude to Richard Krawiec and Jacar Press for the excellent advice and support in editing the manuscript. And much love always to Brian Mc-Dermott, Zoe Pappenheimer, and Leo McDermott for being the lights in my life.

Contents

floors:

&

wilderness:

Life Without Furniture

Housed everywhere but nowhere shut in,
This is the motto of the dreamer of dwellings...
        ~ Gaston Bachelard, *The Poetics of Space*

It has always been this way with the map-makers:
Seaweed starts to burn. Plates shift.

Clouds drift off compass, skew the direction of needles.
always the map-makers: mindful of the edge
of the world and its sailors clinging to it for dear life.

Lost, adrift, skiffs weathered in an ocean's current
or beholden to pine needles, asleep and

dreaming of thick-inked boundary waters
and blue drawings of elephants
tipsy on the coastline.

Those fabled cartographers pinned our *where* to a relief
of crossed lines, tousled vines,
our back porches overburdened with leaves

and there, the last words of crows
dogging us through dusk and the alleyways,
where a puddle trembles of its own accord.

We are here, at least for now. Here and ravenous
for rugs and shelves and soup tureens
and drawers full of matches and twine.

The ambition of curtains, sills, and hardwood planks,
which builds this closure, *enclosure*, this more-than-yourself.
(We are clams; we are oysters with grit in our mantles.)

Oh weary cartographers, slake our desire for the new world:
four chairs, a square. And walls where spiders paint Matisse
markings against a white backdrop.

Always, the cave with its first etchings:

this latitude of light and hair that smells of lemongrass
this longitude of tunneling rain.

rooms

What I Won't Tell Myself

The moon salts the sky with stars and the only sounds in the house
are the dog's breath and the furnace's belch through old pipes.
On this coldest night of winter, I huddle beneath comforters.

On my nightstand, books pile five high, pages bent
at corner edges, annotated, smudged. My young dog twitches a dream
against my calf. I cannot sleep. I'm afraid of how old I've become.

The screens that distracted me all day long with insolent voices
and their bloated sense of significance are now just dark
in a dark room. I suck hard at the air. I'm afraid I've stopped breathing.

A car's headlights skins the bedroom ceiling, leaves blue hollows.
I'm afraid I can no longer cry. When I was a girl, before I'd sleep,
I'd read my mother's girlhood collection of British novels

shivering when the children died from "brain fever"
or "consumption," or when the heroine lost herself
on the wild moor. Mosquitoes needled at my window screens.

Even then, I feared there was no safe place. But I shared my room
with two older sisters whose muffled voices would bring me back
to blankets, sills, the old moon. Back to summer nights

after backyard play when I made sure to unscrew the lids
of jars, so as to return fireflies—those wayfaring lights—
to the space between dark stems, dark blades.

Homing

In this space that has swallowed planets,
that turns me to dust motes, I hone in,
circling, vigilant, looking for home:
a keel, a compass, an anchor.

       A telescope points to the ground.
       the ground points toward sky.
       The limitless plain is lost to me
       Yet, weighing me down, the limitless plain.

       Branches quarrel with wind,
       drop leaves before their time.
       This is my *here*, where the new boots walk,
       where the walkway's re-cemented (gravel
       and chicken-wire to hold itself unto itself.)

A train winks between a memory of leaves.
(Engine whistle through morning yarrow,
blind nose huffing through the scent
of wet grass.) I was so alone in that Jersey field
but peace opened in me like snowdrops.

       Sweet planet of air, I am here! Whatever it means
       to be passing through. Those autumn winds
       so riotous earlier, now diffuse as evening blooms.
       After: fog and mizzle and fumes.

       In this city, a collusion of slick steps, sidewalk.
       This here and now to make a stand, a frame,
       to make my bed. To be stood, understood,
       to know my place. To place the steaming mug down.
       To entreat terra firma: *please know my name.*

Meditation on a Sanctuary

There was the crabapple tree with its scarlet buds,
the cool dirt beneath the LaBelle's rhododendrons,
always cover beneath the picnic table
and sometimes behind the heft of a book
purposely held in front of your face.

There was Grandma's knitted throws and refuge
on the closet floor near battered shoes,
and every box became interior.

And still there is shelter in shade
and pummeling rain, in the produce aisle
with its mounds of lemons, nectarines.

Memory gives refuge. The silver sky beyond the ferry
exhaled a moon. And the mossy graves
tended by tree frogs and ancient red oaks
held stories, indecipherable.

I knew who I was then, brandishing
my guitar, summer bravado and dizzying dunes.

Six blue plums ripen on the kitchen sill.
The oven is turned off, but the smell
of burnt peaches lingers.

Once, I thought I might take harbor in the love
of another. Once I thought that words
could shore up any flimsy, man-made thing.
So where to anchor now? Or whether to?

Rain. The wet moon spills into my garden
and sinks deep, the way of all roots.

Why All The Monks Took Leave from Their Vows

The monks' cells in the Carthusian Monastery
in Milan were the size of a Pittsburgh closet—
cramped, rough-hewn, with only a door
at face-height. Just big enough for a plate of food
to be shoved in and retrieved.

Outside their locked doors, a rose garden
spilled clouds of coral fragrance.
For two hours each day, the monks
were released into open air—
shielding their eyes from the blaze of sunlight—
they pruned and weeded and watered the blooms.

Their vow was total silence,
which included (our tour guide told us)
"no eye contact, talking, no gestures,
no facial expressions," so they might
purify themselves, so they might have
untainted conversations with God.

One monk thrust his nose into every silk
petal as if roses bore the only air worth
breathing. Another monk bled
his thumbs raw from plucking gold beetles
from thorns. A third one was rough
as he sawed the wild suckers from branches.

The sun upon their backs, they drank the salt
of their own sweat, ignoring the others.
And dreaded the hour's end
when they would spiral down
into their griefs and angers once again.

Back in their cells, they tried desperately
to pray. While outside, roses throbbed
and swayed. Anything but silent.

Room in Brooklyn 1932
(after Edward Hopper's painting)

Eloquent lie—shapely white calls the eye into focus,
a vase almost trite in its trill of freesia. Its virtue? A ruse
for the lover who is now just a sleeve
in the sliver of memory she strives to lose. You can't call it *noir*
while she's riveted to the window and squints at the sun.

It was the lure of his facile façade, this lout whose sotto voice
rivered through her veins, his tousled black hair,
and lone-coyote veneer. He was a guise in a suit,
a quitter, a trope. But within her, lust rose
when he covered her cramped living room

in two loping strides. Before she met him, she was unrest
at her window, inert in a hard chair,
her life was a rut of sour green curtains
and shadowy carpet, her tablecloth lost
in its lackluster rust. Back then, women did not quest,

rove, or roam. In her sullen nest, she was elegist
for her own passing life. Love did not enter here
but torque, locomotion. In her borough of lost jobs,
bread lines, and handouts, she boarded that train,
turned her life into a compass, a rig, such silvering speed.

Conversation, New Friends, 61-C Café

New snow—eggs and oranges—
see how it accrues.

I tell of third grade,
how I played with my friends

across lattice-work built
and transformed by our thumbs

and fingers: pulls, over and unders—
the rules deft. *Poems are just artifacts*

that say, "I lived," John talks at me.
His mother's hardwood floor

still full of pins. Her death left him
a house to sell, one blue plate. Artifacts?

Like snow? Or moon on the café's sill?
Like the round shadow deep in the spoon?

Pots of steeped tea. Nails chewed to nubs.
Blue squares of tables and a tiled floor.

Across, his girlfriend, sparkling barrettes,
traces the curve of her ear with her fingertip.

Wind rattles the plate glass. John says,
Baton Rouge and stretches the "g"

like warm taffy. Then Lorca lets loose
in the blustery snow: *I wanted to be myself/*

A heart. John grabs a smoke,
calls over his shoulder, *When do you know*

that you've reached your true self?
Does it matter? What's true? Most people sleep

behind curtains. Outside, sleet falls
slow-motion like pins from her hand.

Window

The whole visible world flows through one white birch.
Blue light in an attic window. Fog blue on the Raritan River.

Little shunt. Conductor. Prisms of wood
refracting every nuance of white. Half-lit rats gleam

deep in squalid tunnels: the ditched apple core
seems fertile. On a highway in West Virginia,

a neon Ferris wheel. Name the landscape of your last hope.
The whole visible world: one white birch.

Your hands on the sleek skin of a man steaming
after an August storm: his silt-green eyes

and cats bathed in streetlight. Sill, frame, smeared
surface. Take your life up to the glass.

Waiting for Gauguin
(after Van Gogh's The Bedroom at Arles, 1889)

His room of vertigo, peeling paint.
Against blue walls, a translucent pitcher,
also blue, a dizzying room, lean-to
walls oppress the pine bed. Caned chairs,
plump and swayed like wheat stacks, sliding down
the too-green floors (the meadows seeping in the cracks.)
How did he ever sleep?

This room so agitated, woozy.
But, too, around the room, the sung strokes
of exuberance, askew, aswirl.
The vibrant calling of a heart so tuned
to vibrations of the cirrus
clouds and the wind drafts of a crow.
Oh there must have been some ecstasies
of knowing? Still the mundane things inside:
pegs, bottles, jacket, stoic mirror
carry on their heated conversations.
while his blanket—florid red,
a raw wound—opens to the light.

Rooms

Music
Bubbling underground pipe. Blue
snow on nasturtiums in early
November. They melt into
a green almost pewter.
And the neighbor stops by to
acknowledge the end
of these prodigious suns
in the grass.

Motherhood
Every night before my
son's birthday, I would stay
up late, hide his gifts,
create a booklet
of rhyming clues and
clumsy illustrations.
He'd wake up gleeful,
reaching for it, off
to his treasure hunt.
This May, he hid the gifts,
and rhymed the clues
for his own son,
turning three.

Beliefs
The earth we love traffics in spirits.
Turn over any rock,
check your peripheral vision
in woodlands.

Death
between gravestones
a wild reclamation
scarlet sumacs, poison ivy
turned tangerine. graffiti
florid on the old brick walls.

Teachings
The language of cities:
gyre and spin on churning gears
rivers muck the noontime skies gray,
slow barge through the locks.

Experience
I have met two beloved ghosts
in my life—my grandmother
who chided me, as I lay
in bed grieving her loss (and
cursing her God.) And my
younger brother who
when I asked out loud
why I still felt him so
vividly, turned on two flashlights
in the tent, then
turned them off again.

Learning
Today I am in my body
all day. Ankles
wonky on the uneven
hillside. Face
toward the seventeen
degree sunrise—happy
and so cold.

Teacher
We wrapped up
The Odyssey yesterday.
18 teenagers. Feasting
on donuts and chocolate
chip cookies. The boy who
dressed as Odyssseus'
sacrificial ram raised
his cup of Sprite to toast
Zeus. He spoke only
in "baa's."

Poetry
For one million poems
I have been trying to tell you
how lonely I am.
No gods left to blame.

Strangers
That stranger's eyes are filled
with ghosts. He is diminished
against the last light.

That woman's baby drools
and chews the end of his shirt.
When I hide my face in my
hands, he knows this game,
laughs before I reveal myself.

What I Thought Love Was
His hand in my black hair
delicately seeking
the ladybug lost there,
offering her to my outstretched
hand, watching me, grinning
as I watched her crack wings
wide and float off toward
an easier sky.

In the Winter Room
(After Andrew Wyeth's painting Groundhog Day, 1959)

Even the light is grimy, less gleam
than grunge. A rectangle of sun
aslant, vectors and angles
in a cold kitchen.

Teacup in its glazed mooring
brims with shadows.
The skate of rim on the empty
plate. February dimmed.

The sun's an old dinghy
without wind. No her.
No him. No yellow dog
sunk into a pillow. Just
a short view

of ragged logs
tumbled where they fell,
unstacked. Within the room,
we miss the arms, the crackling
fire. Instead, the dusty floor.

Is that laughter from the other rooms?
A child clambering
on an oversized chair?
A ladle of beef stew,
red wine in the broth?

This room resists desire
but makes gestures toward a meal
that will be or has been eaten.

One plate is cold.
One knife is cold.
One saucer is cold.
The white tablecloth
is another snow.

doors

Summer Prayer: Pennsylvania
~ in memory of Brendan

We make each other a mooring,
early evening here in the small world,
where gods grumble and root in the dirt
and the red barn molders in summer light,
setting ripe fields to fire.

What we are doing is interpreting
the cirrus clouds, wisps
of names, our beloved dead
who console us with such luminous days
so that we remember them all over again.

The children trail their fingers
in the creek. Birds braid tree limbs
into fluency, while we flicker like old photographs
in the dwindling light. A quarter moon

emerges, a rain halo around it—and you,
my younger brother, my twenty years-gone
companion—flicker on the edge of fire-fly shine.
I breathe deep the soaked wine of fallen apples,

call up your dark curls, long limbs,
your head thrown back in a laugh.
But it is only imagination, summer's limitless
acres. Words cannot bring you back.

But, if words can do anything,
let skies swirl with your memory.
Let it hold you as I can't.
Let them bless this ink with stars.

This Against the Night
   ~in memory of dear Allan

Sweet hyssop and the sweltering hives
from which sail bees, their resolute flight
into July, into my garden. There's a swarm
for the everyday clover. More for the needled
heads of coneflowers. Two more are bristles
past each other in the long arms of the purple sage.

        And on the porch you, a gardener, too,
watch the sky gloom, cloud by cloud. Right now
you want high drama, heat-wracked booms.
The seams of sky and land split, menaced
with the kind of danger that makes you feel
alive. Your diagnosis, new

        and terminal. I kick the calf-deep mint
to fill our noses with it, and mindless, crush
oregano leaves between my palms. I'm usually
good at this, the harder stuff. But it's you.
And from the distance of another year,
I will tell you death is ugly and it's tougher
than last-call memoirs reveal.   And yet,

        I have the shelter of words, of stepping
back into this other scene, the thunderstorm
here now, your grin as rain begins to pound
the petals from the roses. And thunder drowns
my voice, *Hey, come inside—get out of this!*
But instead, your face grows radiant, as you call
back, *God, don't you love it? Don't you just love all this?*

After the Diagnosis

All the subtraction we do here,
reading the dates on the gravestones.

It's June, I muck around in dirt,
plant my million bells, citrus as any blood

orange, a bright border which ants
will travel at great cost sometimes,

like all living things, to find themselves
somewhere else, somewhere kinder.
~~
In the graveyard, Allan looks for turtles,
traces the pond's circumference

scaring red-winged blackbirds
from the cattails. Turtles,

those hard-boxed geometries,
(and symbols of immortality)

are nowhere, not sunning
themselves on logs or pond's edge.

We wander the old cemetery. Allan coughs,
checks overhead: the thunderclouds

are gathering. *My tumors have shrunk
for now,* he says. *Buys me a little more time.*

Frogs startle, a plopping chorus line
from shore and he and I laugh each time;

it doesn't get old. Though Maureen,
my sister, Allan's wife, stops suddenly

and stares into the water, her face
worn silver as thin ice. Thunder rumbles,

closer now, in this summer of unending rain.
Maureen is still a rippling face upon the pond.

And beyond, the waterlilies gape,
petals blown wide.

~ *for Maureen*

Wellfleet, Rain

1.
Under the pine quills, snapped
branches, it's the squish
of mud chill underfoot
that wakes the body.
I am in the fleshy season again.
Sea-salt breath, siphoned
from the roused tides, the heaving
surf, the bay and beach rose,
the un-mowed frenzy
of marram grasses.

2.
When Wordsworth strolled his dazzle
of yellow trumpets in the field,
the jonquils and the daffodils swaying,
it was spring again and soft rains fell.
At that very moment, his feet were solid
on the sure earth, so he praised it all.
But the old poet also taught *awe*,
not just the gentle avowal of beauty
everywhere around us, but the grit
of fear. A potent mix that slid
the hillsides down to sea.

3.
The pour is on. Feel it lash your face?
We carry such pain with us always,
a strange gain. It's been years since
I felt myself beloved. Water falls like typeset
letters: gray, inky, smudged. Misspelled advice.
The sea is everywhere around me, courting
pipers. And late at night, with or without
moon, the forgotten washes in with the tides—
paper boats afloat in gutters
a child's umbrella scuttled by the wind
a snatch of an old harmonica whine
and your tenor singing again—
a long gone pitch and cadence—
which along this shoreline
sounds a lot like rain.

Undertow

When air became water and force dragged me raw against sand
and I tumbled with seaweed, cracked shells bit my flesh
and air became water and there was no time for memories
just fury and force and the steel waves that roofed me
and walled me, that thatched me to seafloor.
The door's key was lost in ruined cities beneath me.
My body was animal—hands clawed against riptide, teeth
clenched, lips glued. I curled like a spiral, an embryo, whelk.

When air became water the sky was denied me, those blues
washed with peach stratocumulus—and gone was the yearn
of horizon lines marking earth/ water/ sea. Just moments before,
laughter rose from my sister, my brother and me, as we splashed
one another, riding swells, as we flipped on our backs.
Then, waves drove me dizzyingly down—no sadness, no fear—
just my thin bones akimbo and my hair whirling up, a black waterspout.
Alone, I was last chapter, scribbling, not even a book—just a concept.

When air became water, I was krill in a blue whale's baleen,
insubstantial, a morsel, a death spiral's captive.
But where was my fear, my final farewells? Where was my fight
to gulp the salt air I loved? Dragged and bruised,
bubbles streamed from my nostrils. My lungs aflame
and my dear heart drummed my ears. Born from the murk
and swelling of tides, I was bright in my white flesh, a sea change
upon me, a small cog spun out, under bray of sunshine.

Crows: The Yard

Here's the digestive maps: tracks of the great
black birds in the snow. You have fed the monks

of the winter trees shelled nuts, sunflower
seed, suet, and they've gone off to pray. The world

blizzards by, whitens like the knuckles of a fearful
hand. You have fed the black-coated warriors

grapes, dried berries, bits of days-old bread, and they
have gone off to battle. February carves itself

ice sculpture. Great clouds of crows eclipse
the falcon's own lonely hunger, which cries out

like a high wind: *Shree! Shree!* The map is a trudged
field, the snow fills footsteps behind you. You fed

the thieving humps, cloaked and hunkered down
in oaks and elms. You fed them all, driven simply

by their hunger, and they circled like a great smoke
ring. Here's the digestible map: the cold world brings

out need, eyes that pierce like stars. You learn to feed
what cannot feed itself, the catcalling monks, the cassocked

friars. Call down the great black fire! Trees will feather into
wings and move closer: the answered prayer, nearing.

Rain, Streetlight
> ~ *in memory of Brendan Fagan*

Puddles like small lagoons. A dog's distant yowl.
Streetlights flare the pavement into dawn. The elm tree's down,

(you were the boy asleep in my lap, that long ride home, little brother.)

dragging splintered branches in the mud, melancholy
as the crows in Van Gogh's final wheat field.

(warm cub! Head of curls. Breathing! I rocked you in the station wagon.)

Why the lightning? Why the sudden flight? Tonight,
you skulked in the pockets of this neighborhood

(mom said, move him over; sleep yourself. It's too long a ride to hold him)

and made this blind alley a vale of the dead. I don't blame you;
rain slipped the snapped trunks, leaves sank, beaten down.

*(I hummed, no one here can love or understand me/ oh what hard luck
stories they all hand me. You curled further into me, kept sleeping)*

It was just a tree uprooted by a storm and could not explain

(such a small story—and yet, and yet—)

why the rainy street turned tangerine with light,
why the old grief smelled of early June: wet earth, honeysuckle.

Poem in Response to Walt Whitman's "The Million Dead, Too, Summ'd Up"

Speak your sorrow to stones,
to creatures hemmed in by highways.
to seawater dashed and daggered by rocks
—such spill, such deluge! The earth is
a deep purse, nursing secrets. Speak your sorrow
to silvering dragonflies over the pond.
How they jazz the waters for their dreams.

From night, borrow cold and the dust
of nascent stars. Head down the trail, wild
and wind-lashed by Hiroshige's rains. Maples red
as life blood will honor your loss in their patient,
timeless rise. Speak your sorrows to torque and drag,
gravity, loft—all the pulls on our animal selves,
our good legs, our soft breathing.

Speak your sorrow to field mud, to cow manure,
to the slight seedlings fledged
and anchor-rooted. The mud knows the weight
and sink of prayers, knows the fulsome swells
of winter snows, the churning green of spring

—and how to cool and hold the fevered spirit
And how to howl its vast release.

Early Spring

What do I ask of the night?
Deer in the graveyard, numinous
streetlight to outline bare branches,
a thick torso of light served up by the moon.

(Inside, gerbera daisies, their color
a pale smear of sunrise. Here,
I'm as certain as rye bread.)

Outside, lonely walks on a street
whose shadows are spent and broomed
into the gutter. My hopes twitter and hop—
layered, dense—an elliptical hedge full of wrens.

(Inside, I am all small, brown birds.)

Outside, the demands
of bulbs grow, break ground,
quiet, insatiable. I teach myself greed.

Silverfish, clay, currents and eddies—who's afraid
of the river of knowledge?

There are oceans that name themselves bodies,
bodies that forget they are flesh,
wet in the flow of the living stream

(bodies that are not just mind, not just
blind intellectual trawling.)

Here's a body, alone, on a walk in deep space.

March and the thickening trees all around,
a dog who lets fly his old fur. It's early yet.
I ask for everything.

The Body Dreams Itself

into an avenue of steam, the streetlights
glow a slick sheen. And down this road,
this August night thick as wet wool, a car
rattles. The body dreams itself heavy,
heavier—into the muscled flank
of a horse straining at a plow and then
it dreams itself a stalk of corn, husked
and kerneled, ready to be pig feed.
The body dreams itself a lime and thus the dreams
are technicolor—scarlet, turquoise, safflower.
(And lost are mirrors, shadows, wavering
reflections in the lake.) The body dreams itself
a postage stamp licked, a dirty sock, the twisted
wires in a phone. It loses its memory
and becomes the flavor of cauliflower, the gap
between a note tweaked from a saxophone
and a woman poised to dance. The body dreams
itself pocked, festooned, dwarfed, and slathered.
It wakes in its own arms,
loose flesh, glass
bones.

floors

The ache for home lives in all of us. The safe place where we can go as we are and not be questioned.

~ *Maya Angelou*

Springtime, New Jersey

1.
When I feel my childhood within me,
it is always Easter Sunday,
rainwater gushing along the curb.

I am all lace, fierce curiosity, alone.
I breathe deep the steamy asphalt, popped
tar bubbles. Under the sycamore,
dropped jacks are tumbled stars.

2.
Rain, rain, rain
savored in the mouth:
The wet and ache
of those long "a's". One letter
in the larger language
of escape.

3.
Earliest memory?
The kith of vowels:
Pith, live, limn, birth.
Grandpa reciting:
bee-loud glade.
The plinth of sentences.

4.
Buttercups beneath my chin testified
to a truth I understood. The world
washed anew by water.

I called this faith. Along with incense
in the aisles and the sweeping
white hems of Resurrection robes.

5.
Deeper than ideas, the blank slate
of streets. Deeper than ideas, a robin's trill
caught beneath my striped umbrella.
Imagination: apple blossoms
swarmed by bees.

6.
Dusk, a drink of blue fog.
Or *twilight*—a silver cave.
Words signaled from shadows.

7.
Olley, olley in free!
The pitch and timbres
behind the bark. And tunneling
through the hide-and-seek shrubs.

8.
Voices echoing back, even still,
call me home. In my mouth,
the sour mash of dandelion.

Hubris

I did not know
anything but that I wanted
to hold his silky
bulk in my small hand.
I made a scoop
of my palm, fetched
the weeks-old rabbit
from the well
of dirt he huddled
in with five siblings.
Above the burrow
dandelions buffed
yellow burned.
His small ears,
skeleton, the fur
against my thumb
the color of pecans.
He shivered and coiled
tight snail-like
nose to tail. I felt such
joy and named him
April. I held his
quickened heart,
instinctual shudder
against a wind
dipping down below
the sunny day's sixty degrees.
Before I found him
the next morning
holding the night's cold
hard in his frame,
I was boundless—
spirit and mother—
seven years old
and god.

Because Desire's Full of Endless Distances
~ inspired by Robert Hass' line in "Meditation at Lagunitas"

Petunias are tenacious, boots and drought,
the trampling of the small brown flock.
Drought or draught. Either way, one winter's night
a deer bent its long neck down to graze in snow
that spilled and billowed from the moon. And each car
stopped on that treacherous hill to watch.

      Like a boat pitched in white caps,
Lady Day sings her blues.

Hopper's seas were always too blue,
too frangible. I could never bear the truth
within his paintings: how no one ever touched,
how sunlight blanched them all and sliced the threads
that joined each one to each.. Until all were adrift
in that sprawl of awful fields.

      Like the 14th century monks at the monastery
in Milan who all went mad, forbidden to share
their lives with anyone but God and the thorns
of perspicacious roses.

Saturdays, this summer, fill will tilt and drift,
The clear-eyed balk of starlings. Even Garamond
left his mark in letterforms: the small bowl
of the *a*, small eye of the *e*.

      Abundance is this yard shot with weeds.
ask rabbits springing from the rhododendrons.
then the string vibrates, copacetic, pulls us
to our feet. But will there be slow dances?
And mouths? Exquisite tracing on the collarbone?

We run on trails because it helps us know our breath.
Tenacity is a virtue. Anger, a virtue.
Impatience? A virtue.

      Lorca said that heaven was *within* the pain,
not *through* it. Oh sweet strings of the guitar
finally plucked again! Hear it in your neighbor's yard?
send the iris. Or the pigeon. Or the peonies—
flushed and open as a child's *Why?*

Quickenings

Crescent dusk, back when possibility
was Eugene and his black hair, earth eyes,

cracking wise, joker in jeans, crooked
grin like a scythe on his face. Oh he could cut
a glance at me that made my knees' quake.

All those quickenings, under the Foley's willow,
its swell of branches covering us, but we only threw

fistfuls of grass at one another and laughed,
chasing dusk to moonbeams
which pooled in LaBelle's backyard, where crabapples

tripped us off curbs. Eugene and his whip-straight
throwing arm. I was terrified of boys and love,

of kisses on the mouth. I was twelve and strong legs
running coltish, catching miles on Overbrook and Starlight,
Cypress Drive, Orion Court. Eugene, that brilliant slice of boy

in summer air, trailed me, honeysuckle 's swoon
perfume. Blue hedges after sunset, when the bats dove down

from steepled sycamores. *Watch out!* Eugene yelled.
We're all after you! and I'd quicken lightly into night.
Fireflies tattooed the air, pulsing for a mate,

those days before love ever caught me,
tackled me, tumbled me long into autumn.

Ode to an Old Lover: The Path, Frick Park

We spilled like the creek running beside us,
down into green canopy, the sprawl of such hush.
Garter snake trail, violets bloomed between roots,

down and my son's bursts of *look!* and his laughter,
his copper hair finding the sun's motes between leaves.
The swelter of city rose low from the weeds and in our woods

a font, a summer baptismal, these trails where you led us—
your black curls and whistles, your three golden dogs
—in the glen where you came most alive—

and my son's green eyes bright and your own green eyes dancing,
and your dogs loud kerfuffle over the hillsides, barking
after squirrels in the tangle of late, lush July.

There was green shade and green air and green gods
among us. And a mossy slick green in the creek's murky bottom.
There was copper and gold giving light to the dappling.

And the sun-fingered branches spilled primordially.
We were here in this moment; we were steeped in the past,
which warmed us, warned us, thick in the swells.

Among these old oaks, my pain was made quiet,
my sad marriage done—but not quite finished (still his plates smashed
against walls, still money fears, loneliness) but all washed away

in this steam bath of air. Ah, love in this green world,
you were more than yourself; I was more than alone;
my son, more than a boy who had just lost his father.

For weren't we, also, a part of such flourishing?

The cascading trills from the mockingbird's songs.
My son filled his pockets with pine cones and stones.
The dogs rose from the creek all goofy and glistening.

And my son laughed again, which was summer to me.
Nothing lasts, I would learn. Our troubles still out there.
But not on these trails. We lay down in the clearing

and saw how the breaking was filled with such sky.
~ *for Michael E. and Brian*

A State of Un-Union

I ache like a radio,
all static waves and sixty-second ads.

I share a supermoon with the west coast
—blue—but they've got blood
moon all tied up this century.

The landlocked kids don't know
the meaning of ebb/flow.

(I drift like an ellipsis,
vanish like a decimal.)

I've been hollow in the shoals
and coltish in the swells.

I've been feckless with some friends
and brackish with the turtle hunters.

The harsh *ck* makes sense when train jumps track.
You almost hear the steel on steel catastrophe.

But then there was the voluptuous rum of our bodies
loving slow between quilts.

A hum before the final shock—two words—
come back, come back.

Naked bulb. Black cord dangling.
Every dream a way back toward you.

Letter to My Father

(in memory)

Of your bread, bread making, of yeast, of salt
and the blue cloth covering the yellow bowl.
Of your hands, blue-veined and shaking
with their own elliptical storm.
Of knead and pound, pound and knead,
of rye and the old table in the old kitchen,
and the fire outside
in the sky, a red torrent, tangerine flares,
of your bushy black eyebrow arched
before telling a joke.

                      Of your joke,
and my laugh, which salts the yellow bowl,
of the blue-cloth, which covers my hair,
and the summer cool of the church
with sun pulsing blue through
stained-glass and onto the hard
backs of the pews, and I've run out
of words for the prayers that aren't
working. *Oh god of the eyebrow
and god of bad jokes!* Did we turn off the oven?
Must it all turn to char? There was fire inside you
(of your bread, your bread making.)
Your legs are now ashes. Your hands,
in red torrent, quake holding the hymnal,
while the choir sings *merciful, merciful Father.*

First Fridays

A girl in the midst of echoes.
Latin rising in a choir of voices,
as I mouth along that dead language,
Sanctus, sanctus, full of roots.
Faith as a paean to vowels,
the rising balloons of *Ave, Ave,*
that tangle with the spilled incense
an ancient musk rinsing all of us,
boys and girls in pews. Inside me,
a deepening well; the waters stir.

I understand little, but it all moves
me to tears. The purple coverings,
when removed, reveal Jesus.
Half-naked, sorrow-laden, bloody hands.
I've never seen such violence, although
I've caught glimpses of the war dead
on the evening news, which my parents snapped off
quickly, shooing me away to homework.

In this ritual of mutability,
the chapel veil shimmers on my hair like snow.
I'm a changeling. An *other.*
A spirit not yet holy.
The priest in his white resurrection
robes lifts his arms, revealing wings,
a dazzling raptor, catching the currency
of wind. And our fervent recitations:
*In nomine Patris, et Filii, et spiritus
Sancti, Amen.* We cross ourselves
over and over, like the damned
who seek their own deliverance.
Wine turns to blood; bread to the flesh.
My eyes are low and seek out shadows.

Our songs are not our own. They belong
to the dead. Our prayers are not for us;
they belong to the dead. Our God
cannot be seen; he is the breath between us
and our beloved dead.
And bathed in stained-glass light,
our faces flicker in golds, reds, blues.
We are the strange and fleeting.
Not from this world or from that.

Pastiche

Sometimes a woman is a cave full of bats,
bats with wings clamped tight,
eyes shut, hanging down.

Sometimes a woman's a birch
without leaves, a stripped sapling
in a black and white photograph.
She is twice removed from herself.

She is netted, pulled from the water, almost
comical in her puckered gasps for air.

Of course, I'm not finding the right words.

I take my seat.

Back in the real world, a kettle shrieks
like wind in a cave. Why shudder
at the underground mouth? It yields
to the pressure of bulldozers.

One person plus one person sometimes
equals a ring of air. An airplane flies by
in a sky green with lightning.
Imagine winging that electric field.

Imagine yourself whole, an unpeeled orange,
the long rind of it.

Even caves fill—with ocean and the long arms
of tentacle creatures. Imagine a woman,
imagine me, the woman of the cave
and all the emerging to do.

And all that arrival.

Driving Home After Singing at Club Café

Tunneling snow, snow blizz, snow blind, snow spires,
snow delft, blue-white like pottery, snow wales

and whirls in winter blur. My lone car slips
down road and slow, alone with my guitar

sprawled on the back seat. Suddenly, between
the recent memory of crowds enthused

applause and Brad's impromptu
jam on saxophone and Jessie's rifts

on the standup bass—
everything's dashed with magic,

magic verged on metaphor. The snow,

a practiced dancer who breaks out from sheer
joie de vivre into a fray of silver

spilling over everything, the maples
black branches now a harbor of white

over the glass conservatory, where inside
the orchids drowse their speckled throats

and tulips, lulled by heat, sleep
near the silent koi. The strong curves

of the road give way to hills and down,
I shift to neutral, pray that I won't skid

past stop signs. As I grip the steering

wheel, I feel my fingertips, their callouses
from steel strings and then I slide.

The snow, glass slivers under streetlight,
a thousand streaming stars.

Longitude

If on a spring night, the moon splits its thin grin
between a last rose glow and the first star,
who's to say it's not a fresh start? Someone yells

from inside Howard's Place, a dive bar on the corner:
First pitch! First out! The grassy field beside it's matted, brown,
still beaten down by months of ice and heavy boots. This old weight

pumps like a heart and not a forsythia in sight. The 61-B exhales
its passengers and smoke into the dusk. Heady, this not-quite,
this precipice, and all along the sidewalks—voices

though the shouts of children quiet down behind closing doors.
Once, my son spent whole evenings on the floor, drawing maps
of make-believe cities, the wiggly blue line of rivers,

the inverted V's of mountain tops and the scrubbed green
of tree canopies. The whole continent situated squarely
by his hand. It was not yet spring then, too, and crescent moons

scythed the light from our skies. Our Shepherd curled
on the fireplace tile. I knew enough, even then—new mother
that I was—to risk desire, greed, to want to hold it all within my hand

and apologize to no one for this:
cartography of the long march, the time passed, the grown, the moved on.

Against Unraveling

Je ne me leve jamais sans me dire:
Tu n'y peux rien: accepte...
                                    ~ Jean Cocteau

1.
Snow again, unnaming everything
as though the tight lines
of an artist's drawing had teased out
to spider's threads and blown
away in the bluster. Turn your face
into it—look up—and you've lost
even the origins of snow. Snow as the source
of all snow. What in the world is as greedy
as these white fingertips grazing
everything at once?

2.
The furred grunt of a dog in my bed,
his belly swirled with thick wool, side
bellowing out in a deep sleep, the tick
and fidget of paws in a dream
and the whole world is a loose canvas,
unstitched. Begin; start anew,
scribble any possibility as though penciling
the flaking pack of a snowdrift.

3.
In our last conversation you said
leave some things to gesture and silence.
I heard, in that moment, the low branch
of a linden unburden itself. And though
I kissed the mossy thatch
of your stomach lightly, the heat
of my mouth found snow
and its inevitable disappearance.

4.
The cemetery's full of small depressions,
sudden sink of boots, enough to snap
your ankle and overhead, snow snuffing out
the small wicks of their names.
My dog leaps and galumphs
through gravestones, tracking
a path from one lost creature
to another, the hard bark
of a stick in his mouth.

5.
This is a March of two full moons.
One shreds down around us, so much white:
paper body, paper woman.

And After We Failed One Another, I Attempt to Define Love Again

1.
Along comes that white haired neighbor
with her goggle glasses sitting ever so straight
on her blue Schwinn, pedaling the long side of sunrise,
apricot glow on her hands, her face, straight ahead,
shoulders back. Light and shadow tryst on pavement and
form a gold-gray river. Every morning, world without end
she rides round and round East End, Peebles, Waverly.
Sometimes a nod, a glance.

2.
My sister, Siobhan, is up ahead, ponytail abob,
back erect as a queen. Sun's brilliant on the East River,
on the bleachers, on the old man's cap and
the sky is blue from car exhaust. I gladly lap
these loops where last night,
Ginsberg's redbrick home (with plaque) stopped us.
And we gaped at the stoop, the dingy snow pile,
and at the steps he had traipsed up and down
for decades, all grit and song
until a guy hollering *Hey, asshole!*
brought us back from our reverie.

We stop for lunch. Siobhan eats sardines
on focaccia, sips pickle soup. I chew olives,
tomatoes, mozzarella spread on toast.
The waiter's hair looks violet in this light. He checks
his teeth in a spoon he's picked up from the floor. And
we laugh with one another, point out plastic flowers
dangling from the fire escape— While nearby at the 92nd
Street Y, Cornelius Eady reads to an eager crowd:
> *And to those*
>> *who defend poetry*
>>> *against all foreign tongues*
> *Love.*

3.
He owned such knowledge of the porous light.
We were talking love, again, me and the artist
with his long white mane. In his hands was the skull
of a possum. He had always collected the skulls
of small mammals and rendered them luminous—
squirrels, rabbits, foxes—he loved their intricate geometry.
Loved the inner sanctum of the bones and how the shadows
made their lonely way along the corridors.

~ for Siobhan

wilderness

The Geography of Solitude

I am here to meet the earth
in the midst of its making.

**

Creek's edge, silver witch
hazel, scales and rust-red bark.
This creek's a small Venice:
all the lit bridges (dropped branches
dropped vines.) Downstream,
I climb all the fallen.

**

I'm an interloper, hushed
by the blown sleet,
the earth's gravitas.

**

Listen, the water's bright vowels
are like chapels washed in blue light.

**

The creek runs white. Clouds sag
along the not-yet May apples.

**

Spring Hollow: scooped oak:
chipmunks gnash within.

**

The past stays past for now.
All along the creek bed, the cycle's
slow tick. Run-off plows
the water tables. The long silver
corridor of March, sartorial and sloppy.

**

Not yet wild onion,
Not yet violets,
Not yet skunk weed,
Not yet poison ivy.

**

Mud sky,
too early to call down
the first geese.

**

If this is loss then let
the wan light compose
the psalms along
the branches staff.

**

This winter slow dwells—
Snow caravan, thicket
of small teeth and tunneled
hovels—to meet now
a slight warmth.
Such silver rain, divided.

No Name Alley

I entered out of simple curiosity, because rain was
                                        pooling there,

because fog had wooled the split
                        fence—into animal—*Mammalia*—

and I yearned to touch its sway-backed spine.
Because touch reminds me I'm alive and venturing forward in a body.

        (Body as paper lantern, body as light beyond bones' blueprints.)

I entered, though there was no drama there, no petty thief's
                                drop-kick-garbage-can-crash!

out of sheer adrenalin joy at getting away

with something in the small shop of human law.
No performance from the make-out queen

and her boyfriend who stocks produce in the market—huge nests
                        of oranges and pears, vine tomatoes—

        (O, to live out all my days within this pyre of soft blue plums!)

                        when he's not unhinging his jaw
                        to kiss his girlfriend in this alleyway.

Alley without name, I enter here to force my hand, to scrape coarse
                        gravel, to skin the bullet of a solo life
                        and find beneath, a child magician

with her one-trick quarter. Here—today—because

        (Another ghost walks next to me, and I, with all my body on.)

Target

Downpour ruckus and we jam-up
by doors that swing open-shut-
open. Soon-to-be-soaked strangers.
Carts brimming. His silver head's too near
my breast: *it's a river out there*, he says,
river out there. I nod and gauge the distance
to my car; I've parked far away
for the walk, *river out there*
and I realize if I don't talk to the old guy
he won't stop. "Yes, a river out there,"
I say. Too curt. But he leaps in,
my feet will get wet. My hair. My arms.
He's a sad Mickey Rooney dancing nouns
past my ears. Then a humming behind us
and a veteran in wheelchair glides past,
hand on controls. Marine cap, Marine blanket
and flag. *He's a Marine*, says the old man.
Yes, I see that! I snap. *I was Army, World War II.*
Never fought. Went to Cairo; it was like a vacation.
I try to get "war" and "vacation" to jibe
in my head. Wonder if only younger women
have old men pour out their small stories to them?
My cart's full of forgettable items. I spent too much
always too much on things I don't need but imagine
will alter my life. *There's a river out there.*

How do we ever bring ourselves to leave
the ordered aisles with their kempt boxes,
clean towels, un-smudged dish sets?
Every aisle's fluorescent with light
and music tranquil as beige washcloths.
We propel our silver carts along
the polished floor until something empty fills.
Outside, what awaits us? *I heard thunder*
in Petco. But nothing like this. A river, I tell you!
I shoot him a look. He's a jittery old man.
I'm a woman whose forgotten how to reach out
to others. There's a river out there
and we're all walking into it, river
out there and we wade in alone.

Nests

All along Pittsburgh's streets—
wigs in the crooks
of branches—beehives,
chignons, hollowed buns.
Honey, this bird has flown!

*

Desolation row, these nests fill with snow, then empty,
fill once more with rain. Tenants left town or chitter in brush.
Nothing sadder than those bald sacks of twig.

*

Something so joyous, you grew wings for it,
stayed open: flight to straw to flight
to long-plucked grasses—you, a streaming song—
a blunt beak, laboring.

*

Harbor of wilderness. Sanctum, sanctuary.
Make no mistake: of wings.

*

Bag of hail!
Bag of air! I am let go of here and there.
And yet, these steady trees hold—

*

Once the young with his
inexhaustible want.

*

I, too, once loved my wilderness.

*

Now, I sit in the gaping mouth.
Open to sky as gray as the sea when it turns
before sunset or a sunset which turns
to a choppy sea. Sometimes—

*

All above these city walks
streetlights gild the ruined village.

*

Through the hours, through these pinholes
 glimpse what fills the nest: filigreed light,
coronas of light, ocean sheen, tangerine tongues
in the dunes. And the most beautiful
which is the most ordinary:
late afternoon sun
on your cup.

*

This empty place is a holy place. It is a place full
of holes. There are days when I curse: nits and chiggers,
unraveling weeds! And days I imagine all abandoned
nests as kindling for all the small bonfires.

*

Oh upside-down bells,
Spring will re-ring you.

Prayer to Dylan Thomas

Give me your street melancholy, your moon rage,
your silence before song. Your lovers abed
and their griefs are long gone.
I'm here in the loud conversations
of those in the coffee shop, traffic
rowdy through too-crowded streets.
Fierce heat turns the haze into white noise.
Red umbrellas crank open
like hibiscus flowers. Black fans rattle breeze
through the air. Heat like a tourniquet;
noise like a dinghy. I'm awash
in these voluble currents. What is art's job?
You wrote for the lovers, the inked sea
of streets, a history of small lives,
of music, of edible wind. Every dark
corner radiated with the touch of your
words. Here, every live thing is loud
with discord. Bring me your silence
before song, your mornings when moon
still holds sway, the hush of cats whiskering
alleyways. Here, even oaks shout with crows
as heat lashes them fast to the branches.

As City Meets the Sea

When the world reshapes itself into coastlines,
a place of straits and river mouths,
bays and beachy backshores,

will we adapt to the increasingly aquatic earth:
wetlands, dunes, and oyster reefs,
the whole visible world floating?

Oh waters of the melting glaciers, oh polar ice sheets
warmed, our modern day maps awash
in high-tide lines (*Don't know why there's no sun*

up in the sky.) And will you find me
with the shark fishermen at the floodgate
waving white flags to Mother Nature and flee

with me, wet with blue rain and leaping
to an archipelago sinking in the sea? No longer
 trying to staunch the natural movement of the sands.

And there we'll swallow down our laughter
as water pools across the mirror. What lies submerged
is loneliness as fluid and fathomless as ink.

As the city meets the sea—storm surge
and plummeted trains—will we ache
with anger at our centuries of hubris?

Here now, in sand dunes forested
with bayberry and beach plum, and wild roses
thick with bees, I am a ferry full of longing

and fierce sorrow, capsized. Knowing tempests
build beyond horizons and knowing, too,
our coveted seashores were simply never ours.

Aphids: July, Pittsburgh

Corralled on milkweed stems by ant rustlers,
aphids the color of mustard,

color of yellow neon signs on a stormy
night in Pittsburgh. A universe I'd easily

have missed, heading downtown, past sites
of closed steel mills. But you're a man who pays

attention to small life—this collecting of sugar water
waste—or other ants excavating pizza crust

on his neighbor's stoop. Everywhere, these wonders:
in the local graveyard, snails crawl upside down

on a pond's surface, cling to the tensile strength
of water; minute islands of duck weed serve as landing

pads for damselflies; jewel weed jettisons seed at the mere
glance of a fingertip. You discover the lone raspberry

bush in a chaos of weeds, broken glass,
empty Iron City cans—and in the suburbs—catch

the doe's eyes steady under hedges. This teeming
world intertwines our lives on Carson Street

besides trains huff and clack, backed-up traffic,
and an old lady who bellows for her cat.

A drunk snores if off on a stoop of chipped brick
sun burnishing his greasy hair. Something to be said

about a man who eases ten bucks into the drunk's
shirt pocket, the small threaded lives.

Aphids on the milkweed, the ants
that labor long in the summer-green universe.

Crows

Black ships trawling a sea of beeches.
Slow vessels. Wind at their backs.

Sails tacked, folded. Their cries crescendo
and 4 PM sets them adrift in a gray,
slushy sky. A December of crows. January.

                    *

A funereal klatch of black-
clad mourners, a murder, thousands
gather on cemetery hillsides, the raucous
din of their laughter. Crow:

totem, trickster,
            intelligent thief, equation
and answer, a jeer cracked open, furniture
for a stripped limb.

                    *

Athabaskan Indians of Alaska speak
of Raven, the Creator, who wailed,
disguised as a newborn child
and was tossed a ball of light
to play with, to quiet him. But he transformed:
all black wings, trumpet *caws*,
skyward bound, above the watery world,
Sun in his beak, the light his great gift.

                    *

Cold and the crows are black hinges
            On the north wind's door.

                    *

Crows, with the afternoon light in their beaks, stitch
a dense golden hem around the top-most
branches of elms.

*

Oh, three-legged sun crow,
      worshipped in long-ago China, feather warm
          rays on us all!

*

Each day, when the light softly
treads across snow, it's the crow who gives credence
to substance and shadow.

*

Roman mythology: crows white as swans
until Apollo, enraged, turned a messenger
crow black as the bad news he carried.

*

They whirl above houses, ashes
blown from a chimney flume.
They are imagination's spark,
dark flame in the dark lake of these days.

*

Crows are not coal or cloak, ink or tuxedo.
They are your overcoat's flap as you brush
past me, leave for good.

*

Snow. Bootprint. Snow. Bootprint. Snow.
Crowprint. Crowprint. Crowprint.

*

Wheelers and stunt-pilots,
diurnal birds of incredible
play, filling the void of this lonely sky.

*

The heart is a crow. A swagger. A gloat
of blue wings. A vase full of night.
The yard's full of corn. Oh, land here.

Audubon's Nature Preserve, Fox Chapel

The sun has left its earth
upon your face, your eyes so green, they leave me
in the wilderness where I first found you,

> arms wrapped around a black oak tree. Geese rumble
> down the dirt away, you're after feathers for a dream
> circle, round birch empty, round

with blue sky on mornings when I wake in the circle
of your arms. Love is a tendering of souls
and a leap into a lake of glass,

> dangers on the shoals, dangers in the depths,
> but I am wet with it, up to my thighs in it, up
> to my nose in it and no snapping turtle, bull

frog, goose, or antlered stag will turn me
back from the kiss above the pines, sweet moldering
in brush grasses, your face above ironweed and vetch

> as you pluck raspberries from stickered
> brambles to pour into my mouth. Five o'clock light
> torches timothy to candles. Deer and wild turkey

venture out, fields pass golden into shadow and a poem
appears in the goldenrod: short, laden, full of pears.
I love you more than I have loved any man

> and the meadows are mad with August. When you
> leave, the sure promise is that summer will escape,
> leak its sunlight into leaves of the deciduous trees

until they flame. Geese will call to one another, refuse
the cooling pond, take flight. The dragonflies mating
will cease, their translucent wings, forget. The moon,

thin as a fish hook, will cast about in a hollow sky.

And Sometimes A Bird Wearing Water and Stillness
~ inspired by a line from Pablo Neruda

Last year, a heron—white reed in the creek—and the yellow grasses around
it pulsed like the sun. Fisher bird, spear. Spike of stillness and focus.
          A one-legged balance,

quiet. quiet. Old creek, this art, in the heat, clumsy movements and slow through
the red clay. Sun on my spoon, on my cup, on the wood of the table.

Dylan Thomas once wrote of his labor by *singing light*
and by this he meant *night* and by night he meant *loneliness*.

Last night, in search of the sky and its Perseid showers, I found the sea
and shark fishermen hoisting the bloody heads of stingrays on their lines,

bait dropped heavy in the new-moon tide, and the tide line swept swift past
the pier—delicate, lacy—the lines drifting into indigo. This night, singing light

swung from weathered pylons: no star flare, no moon. Old sea, this art, in heat
and its charged tides, all the sleeping birds lost in the pines,

and beneath the dark waters, the stirring.

The Hymn of Constellations

Relish whatever lingers in memory:
the 4-AM birds with their songs, stitching dreams
to the waning stars to the sea, to the fog not yet

lifted, to the green field awash in mist.
A bird's note suspends over willows:
moves first toward warble, then arpeggio,

pitch, and tremolo. Waves toss us along.
I try to stop fighting, to just relish the cool weight—
ambiguity—mussing my hair, leaving me

restless at 3AM in dark currents. I have no
grounding claim. I am a parcel lost
beneath clouds, toyed with by wind.

From a round cabin window, I still hear
the stitching songs of the morning birds
and pray they'll call us back to land
where waves plow against pylons.

Far from home and alone, the hymn
of constellations is my only consolation.

Currents sift claws from sand,
clownfish from coral. Something squirms.
Something swims through clean, clear.
Something eyes the depths and dives.

In the city, my footfalls on sidewalks
were so steady. How sure I was then
of my direction. Time shreds and rides like foam

atop the breakers. I dream a home I've not yet lived in:
hardwood floors and brick walls,
the elaborate trill of a bird before sunrise

and those clear notes rising
before morning becomes the only thing I wake to—
my life scrubbed dusky blue—and ends the dream
I cannot recall in the face of such light.

All the Lonely Planets

Between the badly parked car and the red truck, Lao-Tzu contemplates
the diminished world. The tires near him show wear, tread-bare, the white
parking lines thin to gruel. He picks up a discarded popsicle stick, plucks
hairs from his head and crafts a calligrapher's brush, then writes:

The unnamable is the origin of heaven and earth... The garage reeks of exhaust,
rotting leaves. A receptionist, enroute to her office, adjusts her skirt
and is startled to see the poet hunched over his words. Lao-Tzu doesn't notice
her, so intent is he on his brushwork, on the characters building

on asphalt like ancient maps of river routes and night stars. Lao-Tzu trails
his brush, white ink against the blacktop. *Emptied of desire, we see the mystery.
Filled with desire, we see the manifestation of things.* The underground lights are shrill
halogen. The parking garage fills with commuter traffic. Lao-Tzu moves

deliberate through his words, calm as a tortoise.
But, isn't dismissing desire, itself, a stirring?
Doesn't the creation of words fill its own emptiness?

SUV's hulk around him dense as boulders. Car trunks overflow
with empty boxes, old breezes, the stamens of tiger lilies. Who wants to carry
such air and dissipated energy around with them, the miles ratcheting up
a rung-less ladder? Lao-Tzu finishes painting the surface of this parking space.

Nearby, a man parks and pauses to read the poet's words. He wants to pocket
the steeples of stillness he finds there. A woman steps out from her Mustang,
fresh from her lover's morning kisses. She turns away from Lao-Tzu and his words
and closes her eyes to hold onto the full press of memory against her mouth.

Notes:

The title poem "Life Without Furniture" was inspired by Gaston Bachelard's remarkable book *The Poetics of Space*. The title of the poem "Because Desire's Full of Endless Distances" comes from a line in Robert Hass' poem "Meditation at Langunitas" in his book *Praise* (Ecco, July 10, 1999.) The title "And Sometimes a Bird Wearing Water and Stillness" comes from a line in Pablo Neruda's poem "You Will Remember...", which reads "and sometimes a bird, wearing water/ and slowness..." In the poem "And After We Failed One Another, I Attempt to Define Love Again," I quote lines from Cornelius Eady's poem "Gratitude," which is found in his wonderful book *The Gathering of My Name* (Carnegie Mellon Poetry Series, 1991.) My poem "All the Lonely Planets," and the italicized quotes within it were inspired by the *Tao Te Ching*, writings by Lao Tzu, translated by J.H. Macdonald.

About the Author

Sharon Fagan McDermott is a poet, musician, and a teacher of literature at a private school in Pittsburgh. She has published three chapbook collections, *Voluptuous, Alley Scatting* (Parallel Press, 2005), and most recently, *Bitter Acoustic*, winner of the 2011 Jacar Press Chapbook competition, chosen by poet Betty Adcock. Her poems have been published widely in journals including Prairie Schooner, Poet Lore, and Seneca Review, as well as in anthologies, including *A Fine Excess* (Sarabande Press) and *Common Wealth: Contemporary Poets on Pennsylvania* (Penn State University Press.) McDermott has been a recipient of both a Pittsburgh Foundation Award and a PA Council on the Arts grant.

About the Artist

Richard T. Scott is an artist, teacher, and writer working in New York. Mr. Scott has desinged coins and congressional medals for the United States Mint. He holds an MFA from the New York Academy of Art and a BFA from the University of Georgia. His paintings have been exhibited in museums and galleries across Europe and the United States, notably at the National Arts Club in NYC, Le Grand Palais in Paris, and Palazzo Cini in Venice. His work is in private and museum collections, including the New Britain Museum of American Art, the Georgia Museum of Art, the European Museum of Modern Art in Barcelona, and the former British arts minister Alan Howarth.

Among the many awards and grants he has won, Scott was selected as one of "25 Artists of Tomorrow" by American Artist Magazine, was inducted as a "Living Master" by the Art Renewal Center, and received a grant from the Martha Boshen Porter Fund. He has been published extensively, most notably in American Arts Quarterly, Hi Fructose, The New York Times, NPR, and Radio France International.

Scott has given workshops and lectures at the Tyler School of Art, Lamar Dodd School of Art, the Florence Academy of Art, Laguna College of Art and Design, the Lyme Academy, and the Wethersfield Academy, among others.

He is represented by Galerie L'Oeil du Prince in Paris, France and Spalding Nix Fine Art in Atlanta, GA.

www.richardtscottart.com